THE LONG COLD GREEN
EVENINGS OF SPRING

The Long Cold Green Evenings of Spring

ELISABETH HARVOR

SIGNAL EDITIONS IS AN IMPRINT OF VEHICULE PRESS MONTREAL CANADA

ACKNOWLEDGEMENTS

I am grateful to the Canada Council, the Ontario Arts Council, the Toronto Arts Council, to B, C, D, F, R, Sarah, and T, and to two Michaels: Michael Redhill who edited a previous version of the manuscript, and Michael Harris, my long-time editor at Signal Editions, who (along with Simon Dardick) generously made room on the Signal Editions list for this book. Thanks also to Carleton University, the Ottawa Public Library, the University of New Brunswick, and Concordia University, all institutions whose invitations to be their Writer in Residence for four- and five-month periods between 1993 and 1997, gave me extra time to work on the book.

The poems in this collection first appeared in *Quarry, The Malahat Review, The American Voice, Poetry Canada, Prairie Fire, The Antigonish Review, The Fiddlehead, Yak, The Pottersfield Portfolio*; "Saturday Afternoon at the Clinic" also appeared in *Sudden Miracles,* an anthology of the work of eight women poets. "The Other Woman" appeared in both *The Antigonish Review* and in *More Garden Varieties,* one of the League of Canadian Poets' anthologies of prize-winning poems.

Véhicule Press acknowledges the support of the Canada Council for the Arts for its publishing program.

Signal Editions Series Editor: Michael Harris
Cover design by J.W. Stewart based on photographs by Mark Garland
Photograph of the author by Andrew Chomentowski
Typeset in Perpetua by Simon Garamond
Printed by AGMV Marquis Ltée

RSN - 18032

CANADIAN CATALOGUING IN PUBLICATION DATA

Harvor, Elisabeth
  The long cold green evenings of spring

Poems.
ISBN 1-55065-091-2

  I. Title.

PS8565.A69L65 1997   C811'.54   C97-900452-7
PR9199.3.H3615L65 1977

Published by Véhicule Press, P.O.B. 125, Succ. Place du Parc , Montreal, Quebec H2W 2M9
Distributed by General Distribution Services, 30 Lesmill Road, Don Mills, Ont. M3B 2T6
Visit the Véhicule Press web site: http://www.cam.org/~vpress

Printed in Canada on alkaline paper.

To the memory of my father

CONTENTS

The Damp Hips of the Women

THEY'VE FOUND A SHADOW

An ex-husband waits for a lab
report, winter, final decade

When he calls to tell me
his news (they've found a shadow
the size of a blurred grape in a lung)
I'm made ten times more mortal,

mortal by marriage,
I add up the years we
breathed the bad air
of the century

and after the doctors have
opened his chest in the nearby
hospital it used to amuse me
to call the Staph House

I picture a nurse
as she draws his wrist
in a low lift to her hip

so she can hold it,
pressed into the throb
of her listening stillness

while she lowers her eyes
to take a careful count
of his pulse.

I'd hate
above all things
to be in his place,
flat on my back and
made to feel what's important
is best politely forgotten,

to say nothing of my aversion
to bad food and pain,

(unless it's really
my ashamed love of pain)

hate to lie clamped
to the bed destiny
keeps always unkindly
in wait for me, hermetic
world organized into orange juice
and terror, bent glass straw
poked into ice chips,

distancing tinkle
of glass trays and needles

(hope, as usual,
precipitating sadness),

hate to get weepy
but afraid to let anyone
in power know it, hate to

regret things, I wonder if he does—
two days after the surgery his doctor
brings him a gift: a briefcase
made out of clear plastic,

drainage tubes
from the stitched
lung feed into it,

bubbles lift,
then slide back

in the tubes
when he breathes

(our sons tell me this—
they looked straight down
through his briefcase to
watch him breathe
in and out),

and so now when
he is up and about
he carries

a cargo of discharge
instead of papers and notes.

I picture him at night
as he totes his clear briefcase
filled with tubing and breath,

I see him pace off
to meet death (or a new life)

all the way down
to the end of the Fell Wing,

I see him look down to admire
what's three stories below
the tall windows of dark:

the grass and concrete
arrangements of the hospital park.

THE DAMP HIPS OF THE WOMEN

Two weeks before
the end of the war
with Japan, I climbed
with my mother and four
of her friends up the path
from the beach, up the long
aisle of shivering poplars,
I remember spandex
and paisley

expanding, contracting
on the damp hips of the women,
but it would have had to be some other
fabric back in those edgy days of

pale sunshine and fog—not spandex
but some sort of elasticized jersey,
the air smelling of decay, effervescence,
damp birth or death of the earth,

one of the women walking
with the arms of her orange cardigan
tied into a broken-necked knot
on one hip, making her oiled back
end in an uneven and cocky orange apron
    worn backwards
its jaunty sway back and forth

and me with a river
of sand embedded in the
flowered crotch of my swimsuit
    along with a deeper
worm of wrong down in the divided
pudge between my babyish thighs;
    my body
feeling shivery, peppy, as if it
could make me want to cry out "I love you!"

(or "I hate you!")
or suppose I had startled the world
by yelling out "Hip!" Would the women
have waited then, for two more hips to follow?
And for the two hips that followed
to be followed by a shy and frail hooray?

Or I might have shamed myself
utterly by crying out *breast!*

At nine, I couldn't imagine
ever being anything but a lover
of women, I loved the way
they smelled of the hurtful
suction of their wet bathing caps,
their earrings

pressed tight
to their ears by their
white rubber bonnets,

loved the way they
kept swinging backwards

into the river,
sinking slowly back
into deeper water

to laugh
like women in love

at the dipped
coldness,

loved their yelps
of belonging laughter,
loved the slits of winter-white
skin that flashed from the tops
of their brown thighs as they sat
and smoked out on the end of the dock

and then bent over to cry out,
helplessly caught in the adult pain
of amusement, loved their nailpolish
and the sun-paled tan

weave of their borrowed
sandals and their bracelets'
jingles, loved their lives.

◆　◆　◆

Somewhere, beyond sky
or river, they are all

still in their damp swimsuits
and still all laughing and climbing
up into the grove of excitable
poplars, mounting the path
in sprung single-file.

But no, it's before
even that,

the long afternoon
graduating itself into twilight

while the five
are still holding out
at the far end of the dock
for a final low gossip,

that last peaceful malice,
wigwammed by towels, a last cigarette.

WE HAVE FOUR HUSBANDS

We have four husbands
between us, most of them Emily's,
and she is such a boy of a woman,
with her own-the-world walk,
her unrehearsed smile. As we
climb the frozen path to the Lodge
she tells me tourists can take
tea there during the summer,
tea for a fee,

and she points out the cairn
where the architect's grave is.

Lost in a field of the fallen
grass of November, it's across the
dirt road from the kitchen garden,

now only a bouquet of bare branches,
snowed in at the roots, but in summer,
says Emily, it'll be blooming with herbs
from the nineteenth century.

We talk of mothers and others,
although mothers most

(how much Emily's mother
is like my mother, how much
two of Emily's husbands
are like my ex-husband,

how much all four of the husbands
are like the two mothers),

we also talk of a book Emily
is reading, on quantum healing,
on mind/body medicine,

she tells me about something
called "the impulse of intelligence",
which means, she says, that a thought
and a molecule are tied together.

Like a husband and wife?

"Perhaps," says Emily.
"Although a better analogy
would be a two-sided coin.

Once the impulse has
started to rise, there is
no turning it back,

the thought is
the molecule,

the molecule
is the thought."

Plunged deep
into molecular thought
on the theme of my life,
I think of words a person
might want to take back,
and the fool I made of myself
with a certain someone,

on paper too,
and only last summer,
and how, when I asked him
to please let me have
my mad letters back

he said no, they're mine,
you gave them to me,

while we gazed at each other
with the lively and cold
gaze of true lovers.

I think, too, of wedding invitations

mailed off
in the bridal deep-freeze
of a January morning years ago,
this is what walking can do
for a person, so much time to brood,

I'm thinking, too,
of a woman friend who has
recently made me extremely
angry and so I think *yes* as Emily

points to a look-out that will
be breezy on even the hottest day
in the summer. Which makes me
wonder if my kind of anger isn't

after all a minor emotion.
And why do I need friends who
will honour and cherish my
little rages against friends? But

      I do.

Standing alone
on a long slope of snow
there's a lonesome dark tree
and I wonder if it was a woman
who was too sad in an earlier life
and so now is doomed to live out
a life of karmic correction
disguised as a tree.

But now we are on our way
down to the zoo, and Emily speaks
of being a Buddhist and I am quiet
and on guard, the way I always am when
someone speaks to me of faith and belief.

As if what I fear above all things
is some sly sideways dose of spiritual
instruction. And now we are down
at the buffalo compound,

the buffaloes brooding piles
of manure and caked fur

on their high-heeled
hooves in the mud,

practising stillness,
the whole Buffalo family
in training to spend eternity
over somebody's fireplace.

Then it's across a field of snowed
    stubble and down
through a white wood and back to the city.

On Emily's street, I tell her
of the fight I've been having
with the aforementioned and unfair
woman friend ("I see her as my mother,
she sees me as her mother").

How does she take this, Emily the Buddhist?

"Of course, a Buddhist would not approve,"
I say, with a disdainful but also quite
worried grandeur, "of all this anger!"

But Emily, up on her verandah by now,
smiles down at me from above the
whitewashed gingerbread trim
of her pulpit and I think, Oh God,

here it comes, some
sanctimonious bromide
from the people who giggle.
Or are they the other ones,
the ones with the small drums

hugged up high
between armpit and heart?

The ones who dance,
the ones who ebb in and out—

"The Buddhists say...."
says Emily, and she's
smiling as she must

have smiled when she
was a child and held up a finger

to say "Confucius say...."

but what she says next is:
"The Buddhists say that
anger is very intelligent. Because it
makes us see things as they are."

"As they are!" I echo,
walking backwards, and in so doing
almost stumble
      (also backwards)
            down the steps of a karmic
                 correction disguised as a stair-
          way carved out of stone. But I
              do a quick

                  (backwards)
swerve and rally to
cry "As they are! Yes! I believe that!"

It's a fine new
possession I carry
home with me, her saying that,

as they are
as they are

SATURDAY AFTERNOON AT THE CLINIC

The only patient,
I study the reproductions—

Monet at Antibes: the blown
spring-to-the-hilt
havoc of it,

all wreckage and blossoms;
also one of Van Gogh's bedrooms—
the one at Arles, maybe,

making me think
of another bedroom,

splintered blue-green
of the child-like wooden bed,

picture's basin and jug
chopped out of blue paint,

ordered alternative
to Monet's reckless springtime,

framed,

windblown
taunt behind glass,

plunged light
with its message:

This is the world!
The world you should have chosen!

Not these public
armchairs

not this clinic among leaves

I look until I can't
look any longer, then out
of apprehension

pretending
to be boredom

set myself
an assignment:

Compose ten
phrases making use
of the word *only*—

To begin: My husband,
long ago, posed stiffly
beside me while a burly

man in a smock
embroidered with a
bunioned black cross
made out of x's, is speaking
of 'this woman', asking him
to vow to cleave *only unto her;*

Next—but this is years
later—a clear male voice singing
a song beginning *Only the lonely,*
making an arch of pure sound
high over his own life—

After this, someone saying about
someone: *Only three months to live.*

Then there are all those
moments of misplaced trust in Fate,

someone speaking
of someone who only
ran out to the corner store
for a minute to get some nutmeg
and cleanser, but then:

the bomb fell,
the gas main exploded,
the house burst into flame,
it only took half an hour
to burn all the way
down to the ground

Only the children
were home at the time,
they had been told to
only play quietly,

to not light the candles,

the littlest girl only
wanted to see what her sister's
braids would look like

burning

(she was only four)

Only tell me this:
what wrong turning
did I take in my life
that I should find
myself indoors

on a day
such as this one?

The grass the healthy green
of the grass in a graveyard?

The strong
sun burning down?

Somewhere
out in the world

cold lakes are
throttling

the plunged
sound of men's
laughter

hot summer winds
are bathing

some women's skin

A Propos of the Snow

SNOW AND THE END OF CHILDHOOD

We sink up to our knees
in its cold fluff

and deeper

until we're
stopped short by it

and there's nothing to do
but fall face-down on it with a

sapped joy that feels sexual…

But how is it that we've been brought here
to the dark edge of finding? Losing?

Sleds drawn in impatient jerks
behind us,

disobedient dogs.

SNOW AND MOON RIVER

Looking down on swimmers
swimming in what looks like
a greenhouse for swimmers

Now that it's dark
and snowing again,
this morning's snow,
seven stories below
on the roof of the tower's
glassed-in swimming pool,
has been turned into
black jungle foliage,

swimming-pool-lit
green glass beneath it,
the pool now and then
given a disciplined wobble
by a swimmer, human torpedo
aimed through the lime depths
of chlorine and water.

Snow falls on snow,
snow falls on the swimmers,

farther west,
where the one-family houses are,

snow must be falling
on the tree the City beheaded,
all afternoon I've been telling myself
I should walk there, walk to my tree,

but I've been too afflicted by Sunday

(forty-five minutes to pull
on a stocking)

(another hour and ten minutes to
take three sips of cool tea…)

But now I know I'll
die if I don't
get a move on

and so I shake myself
into my coat and go

down and out,

step out into the frozen swept air,

new snow still falling
like a thoughtless promise from God
that can never be broken——

turn up my collar
and hurry the six blocks
to the street where my tree
is still holding its
two long arms

so beseechingly out,
its stump of neck
tinctured black,

while under its cravat
of curdled wood,

someone is waiting,
standing and waiting,

an old woman in a long coat
is standing too still

under the left arm of the
frost-cracked headless tree.

My feet get a cringe in them,
but keep on walking,

even though I know
she'll tell me something
I can't bear to hear,
but when I get to

where she waits
she only tells me she
can barely walk, her
feet and legs hurt her
so. I crook my right arm
and when we make a slow

procession through
the falling snow to the
street where she lives
with a woman who is, she says,
sometimes cross and

sometimes kind to her. I
ask her if she has always
lived in the city—thinking,

with the usual
terror, how do people
end up where they end up,

in single rooms
in the houses
of strangers who
are sometimes cross
and sometimes kind to them?

But she tells me she was
born in Moon River. And when I say
"Oh! Like the song!" then ask her
if Moon River's out West

she says, "Don't know.
Don't know, my darling—it was
a long time ago."

HER CHILDREN OR GOD

In the singing cold silence
they're not speaking again
while the snow-meringues
and ice-biscuits that roof
the winter-loud brook

decide to stay with us
all the way out to the highway,
we three prim with fear
in our new winter coats
in the freezing back
of the car,

stiff arms
poked so deep they're
almost drowned in our pockets
while we stare out at the cold fields
as if they sadly displease us.

When we reach the steel bridge
that's painted the same green
oxidized copper gets

after years of exposure
to rain or blue sky, the car

skips onto a patch
of black ice so that
our father is thrown
into driving like a

deranged skier
while our mother's

caged whimper
backs her up
against the chrome rib
of her door handle,

her cry
preserved in the silence
of the next thirty-five miles,

her craving for life
an embarrassment to all,
since it seems she is forever
proving with her unkindness
how much she doesn't value it
with the necessary tenderness
towards her children or God.

COLD DAY IN AUGUST

In the sun-pen
our father built for her
so she can start in on her tan
while there's still snow
on the ground, she's
flat on her back up on the
slant of roof that looks down
into the snowed-in
back garden.

It's still only March,
but already hot, the roof's
asphalt shingles smell of tar
and burn through her back,
she must feel it, that painfully
coarse industrial sugar,
while high up in the woods
the farmers are making their way
down our ice-aisle between pine trees,
fragrance of torn tree-skin,
strapped leather

down the steep
lumber road from the bluff,
their jingling horses

dragging the final chained logs
along the pegged ache of the winter.

These men must get a nearly
aerial view of her, our little mother,

tiny naked penned woman
turning pink to the

jostling and high sexless
chime of the bells' little jingles....

◆　◆　◆

But was she a tease? Afraid of sex?
Pretty woman who shone and shone

until there were no
scraps of leftover light
for her two daughters?

Who now sit, locked in a car
on the ferry sailing out to the Point,

all around us the bay's
broken bracelet of islands,

their steep walls
of trees

knitted into
a sketched darkness
by someone who must have
kept whispering, You will
learn nothing here, there isn't
even the relief of a meadow—

only the monotony
of island,
island,

crowded spruces
and cedars,

only grey water lapping

at eroded tablets
of rock, shored up by grey
pebbles and the wetter

smaller pebbles at the ledge
of blacker, deeper water

while we, now mothers ourselves,
pull all the bad old words
("narcissistic," "hostile")

out of the family hat,
the tea in our thermos
tasting of tar and old smoke.

But how sad and thrilling
these little talks are!

Sad and thrilling
and almost erotic, I can
feel the sex of them, two inches

down the inside of each thigh,
the fine wince of the personal,

all this is in August,
cold day in August,

rain coming at us
over the darkening water.

Before we reach the far shore
it hits our windshield

in an aimed scatter,

but as we turn,
wheeling,

all the while
treading water

while heavily shedding it,

the storm comes
at us from behind,

attacks us full-force
on the car's long-eyed back window—

Even so, it's still
the comforting
and privately

historical
assault of the rain,

its little winter

Snazzy Night

SNAZZY NIGHT

Snazzy night,
and the air rings
with arrival

down the long tables
cooked trout

sweet as sand

and our mother's
mad salads served
with her voice

calling out over
all the candles'
arrangements of flickers,

Don't eat the rhubarb
leaves, they could kill you!

Tall women float down
to tell us, "Now you are tall!"

And when they pull our faces
hard to their cold satin lapels,
their cold jewelry hurts us

while out in the tamed driveway
dark smiles keep stepping out
with the twilight.

Cruel, some of them,
bitter largesse—

We see two of the women
exchange theirs above a cream sauce.

When we understand
it's our mother they're mocking

we long to run to her,
swift with bad news,

we'd do it too,
but at this moment
we see her turn to

laugh and the light scatters

and so we stay where we are.

Soon there will be music,
its near and far cry.

TRIAL BY FIRE

I. AMMUNITION

After winter rain,
the hill of snow

west of the Kiln Barn
turns into a mound
of thumbprints

hardened into ice,
while inside the Work Room
where it's dryly dusty and warm,
our mother's thumb scoops
and presses, making a balaclava
of blunt scales all the way
down the mounded hill
of her clay

until it becomes
the head of a woman,
the eyes eyeless,
skinned almonds,

now she is using a chrome pick
to poke a decimal point

into the circle for each iris,
and so now they miraculously
appear to be able to see, the eyes
of that stern and unbaked little
cloaked woman, and if she could really see,
she'd see out to the tall row of gas tanks
capped by snow and parked next to the Kiln Barn,
she'd see that they are her saviours, her three
silver transformers—belted and lethal,
they're standing out in the

windy March night,

rained on and snowed on
in all the bad weathers,

ammunition for the blowtorch,
its unendurable fire.

2. PARENTS

Everywhere war,
even a pyramid
of clay cannons

lying in wait
to the right of the wheel,
but now they are days and days
behind schedule for the big firing,
our unhappy father and mother,
and the air is painful,

coldly electric with blaming,
our father slumped with an
awful sadness at his wheel
as he kicks with one foot,

raising tower
after tower to shine
and spin to its height,

our mother
perched with her
forbidding silence
up on her stool beside
her clay self,

her tray laid out
with its delicate
instruments of torture
(given to her last Christmas
by our family dentist).

Like one who will never
find it in her heart to forgive,

she picks up a pick
and engraves a blind plate with it,

precisely making
her marine and botanical
incisions: vines, blissful fishes,

while back at the house my sister
and I are vowing to make marriages
conceived in true love as we wash the dishes.

LEAVING HOME

Leaving home to go to
the doctor's house

The ferry's great
paddlewheels

keep threshing
the river

into river

so that it falls
and re-falls

down

tipped
shelves of water

while sunny islands
bob by us

each one equipped
with a miniature road
and two houses

bright histories of weather

farther out in the bay
the islands are small

and then even smaller

frightened groves
of trees

riding
the darkening water—

It's endlessly deep here,
the river's

hills of trees
don't have any beaches

only their claws
backed up from the rock face

or else
dividing it

going down and down

THE GENDER OF THE HANDS OF
WHOEVER COMES WALKING

At the doctor's house:
pneumonia at fourteen

Someone comes in
in the dark to lay a
cool hand on my forehead.

The doctor's wife: I can't see her face,
I can only see the face of her watch,
set in its band of silver scales

and gleaming selectly
in the hallway's faint light.

Now and then the doctor
comes too, to give me my shot,
although often the shot is given
to me in my sleep,

a bee sting in a dream
in which, perspiring and desperate,

I'm climbing a hill or running.
Then someone is coughing
and I wake up shaking

and frightened to see
a man's face looming horribly
above a small flashlight.

I can hear a nurse
is with him, I can hear
a wind in the starch of her apron
as she walks, I can see a

watery gold hoop
of light reflected high up,

the way it keeps wobbling
close to her apron's waistband

as she bows down in the dark
to hold a small glass with a

clear syrup in it
pressed to my lips.

"Linctus codeine," I hear
the man say, "it'll do the trick
every time." They seem to be
such a tight little unit,

even closer than lovers
and after they leave me, I sleep
for what feels like many days and nights.

I dream about the early days
at the doctor's house, dream
of the wall of yellow leaves

hiding the houses the
hospital rents out to the nurses,
dream of a windstorm that

blows all the leaves south,
so that the following morning,
hurrying to school,

I can see into the sunlit backs
of the nurses' gardens, but then I am
all at once at school, as if by bad magic
I am at school and I am supposed to
know the answer to something and don't,
and one of the doctors comes
into the classroom (but by now

it's the examination room,
the examination room
with my bed in it,

I'm the only student
who will be writing the exam
from a bed), the doctor
tells me I'll have to

drink a cup of hot ginger ale
and then some people are

laughing and I want them to
stop because the noise is

making my throat hurt.
But then the days turn into
days again and I begin to be aware
of the gender of the hands of whoever
comes walking through the sanatorium gardens
to give me my shot. Most often

it's a cool dry male
hand that shoves my nightgown
high up on the brow of my hip,

then presses the hand's heel
against my hipbone

while the thumb
makes a decisive

compass swing
down my right flank to
locate the point where the
injection is to be given.

My buttocks,
being assessed for the shot,

feel suddenly shy
as if all my bashfulness has
rushed to collect itself down in them.

There is something
shamefaced too, something
with too much shocked
self-rebuke in it,

in the quick way
the doctors yank down
my nightgown after the shot.

It's as if my shyness
makes me unworthy
of their shyness—

as if my shyness is
only childish and silly,

while theirs is tensely
adult and aloof.

With a winced thrill
that above all seems to

crave to keep itself
down in that part of my body
where I feel it the most,

I dwell on that embarrassed
male quickness all

the long afternoons.

THE DARK CLOUDS BETWEEN THE RIBS

In the toppled
cold of a morning
cool with promise as
the morning of the first day
in a foreign country, I sleep,
then throw up in my sleep, when I
wake I feel a network of vomit
in my hair, a web of stringed milk
and corn kernels.

The doctor's wife,
a reserved woman, rebukingly
fragrant, bathes me, washes my hair
in the tub. I am apologetic, I am
grateful for everything

she does for me, I want to
thank her, but right away it's too
late for thanking, and then in no
time at all there isn't a word

in the world it isn't too late for.

Still, I do think
of possible words to say
at the same time that I know
any word I might throw into
our great roaring ocean of silence
will be the wrong word,

no good word will do,
no good words will come to me,
only a wash of bad words
with their hiss of *say me, say me,*
and yet silence isn't
the solution either

because the more
I don't speak,

the more violently
my heart beats.

And what if there's a bad word
I am simply forced to shout out?
A word so wrong it will ring, evil bell,
toll in the clear air forever?

But now I am better, now she's
carrying my supper tray up to me
at the same time the nurses are
bringing trays to the patients
across the dark lawn from the
doctor's lit villa. I become
an eating invalid watching
other invalids eat,

spooning up soup or pudding,
I have a pleasing image
of the sanatorium on these
spring-brilliant nights:

a dolls' hospital
facing a dolls' house.

It's my last time
before saying goodbye forever
to the perfect safety of something—

sickness or childhood,
I can't quite tell which.

But now the Bay of Fundy
seems more of an ocean than ever
in the suddenly warm

and hazy spring weather,
when I get out of bed and
go over to the window to

inhale the blue
hyacinth, blurred

beacon of fierce sweetness
on the warm windowsill

and look down
at the rock garden's boulders
losing their Japanese markings of snow.

It's foggy the morning
the doctor's wife takes me over
the dewed lawn for X-rays,

there's the smell of the steam
from the sanatorium Laundry

in the fog but no shrapnel bits
of light or black or whatever it is

they're looking for in the dark clouds
between the ribs, I'm to be allowed
to go home for the Easter holidays.

The morning of our journey
I wake to find damp blotches and scars
of rust all over my flowered pyjama bottoms.
I don't tell the doctor's wife.

I hide the bloodied pyjamas in the hamper
to be wheeled off to the sanatorium Laundry
where they'll be harshly disinfected with the
tubercular linen. This isn't the first time

I've tried to hide something
from the doctor's wife, the nights
the doctor used to take her

out to the Union Club,
I'd slip into her room to

breathe in the preened aroma
of fur coats, fur jackets,

in her coach-lamped mirror
I'd pull on her skirts, pose

lips and cheekbones
above the silken sag
of draped blouses,

toss my hair
to fill up my eyes
with adulthood.

Nobody knows this,
not even my brother,
carrying a basket

of hard-boiled eggs and bananas
out to the car in the dark.

The doctor's wife
turns the door key, the car key,

we drive past blinkered
groceries, locked drug stores,
the whole city dull with cold, sleeping.

Dead to the world in the back seat,
my brother can't see the way

the Bay of Fundy's horizon
keeps offering eye-pain and brine
with its silver, can't see how

overnight the city's poor outskirts
have been turned into a town

felled by dawn in occupied Europe.
We drive down a highway whose white lines
keep joining and breaking beneath us,

we drive down a paved road with no white lines
running down it, we follow a truck

with a horse on its back
up the plank hill to the boat,
the doctor's wife peels the
napkin back from the basket, the
dill pickles are alligators with no legs,

warted emeralds, the farmers
stand posed to the wind,

hard hands muffed
high in their windbreaker pockets,

the boat flushes itself backwards
out of the docks of small islands,
ferries its way across the

chopped grey of the bay,

churns up the aisle
of still water

between breakwaters
weathered as gallows.

The deck-hand ropes a pier,
quick as a fish darts

to harpoon the mainland.
He's a boy my brother and I
have known since we were babies
but our absence (and the doctor's car)
have turned us into people of glamour.
As we are inched in privileged shame
toward the ramp he pretends
not to know us.

A dovetailed squeak,
tamed jolt of landing,

then it's uphill onto wood slats,

wrenched
scurry of gravel.

Out of nowhere: nausea—
the homecoming longing

not to feel longing. We drive
until the wooded hills are dull headaches,

with a sickening turn,
we turn down a track whose
parched mane is a long tuft of grass
stained by lye and dogs' urine.

We reach the house an hour
before lunchtime on a

winded March morning

and it's still the same
and more than the same

(beloved, terrible)

we pass through the iodine
smell of the old shed

where the bicycles
are stored until springtime.

Dead world!

After we've eaten,
my mother takes me aside
to say she hopes I am

grateful to the doctor and his wife
for all they have done for me
always—

I go up to my room

I sit a long time
on the side of my bed

I think of youth,
I think of how eternal it is,
I think of how it just

keeps going on and on
with no let-up

In the Cold Sunlight

ONE OF THE LOVESICK
WOMEN OF HISTORY

Do you want to know what he's like, my boyo Maurice?
Well, he's a swine, and a this, and a that, and even
a cute little fellow, and a skin like satin. That's
how deep I am in. I kiss you, dear heart. And I kiss
you again....
                    —Colette, in a letter to Marguerite Moreno,
                         June 21, 1925

She can't get up out of bed
for wanting to be in bed with *him,*

the morning's windy,
windy Sunday, the wind plunging
the trees to their knees,

then right away up again
to fly-cast their spotted shadows

down half of one wall. She's
thinking of their difficult history

and why she ought to be glad of it;
of how it's meant she can't wait to be
honest with him, to make up for all the

ways they've misunderstood each other,
what they've put each other through.

Lying in the small room at the back
of the house, she keeps seeing his eyes—

the trick they have of taking
her measure, even in absence.

The wind's not so wild back here,
only the back and forth creak of shoes

high up in the house-bones.
But there's a word for that—
for that part of the walls where the wind

keeps squeaking its way in and out.
Something swain? Swainscotting?

No, swain is a lover.
Swain and swine, now and forever.

Dearest Swine: she can see herself
as one of the lovesick women of history

sitting formally down
at her sunlit desk to write that.

Dearest Swine: I hate and love
and hate and love you.

Except that you can't call a man Swine
unless he's given you grounds. But he has,
he has given her grounds—

the way he has looked at her,
the way he has not looked at her,

the way he has looked
while pretending not to look at her.

Isn't this giving her grounds?
To imagine touching his face?
And aren't the shy beginnings

the best parts to dream of? (Although
it's true that last night, thinking of him,
she fell asleep to—*from!*—thoughts of touching

much more urgent parts than this. But now,
out of cagey hope, it really is only his face
she imagines: it's nosing its way to the waiting

drooped bird of her hand,
a cat nosing with drunken mad love
a stranger's nearest finger.

A love affair between a face
and a finger. Or a bird and a cat?
No, don't think of that.

But the fear is a lover's fear—
the fine old grand fear of falling,
and when all's said and done

a small price to pay for being
given so much to hope for.)

She gets up, she ties on the slinky
robe with the fling of quicksilver
seas and planets rolling on it.

From her high galley kitchen
she can see the way the trees are

tossing their green hearts
to the wind. Any minute now she's
due to tell herself: Don't be a fool.

Until then all she can think is:
What you want to have happen can happen.

IN THE COLD SUNLIGHT

There's the distant clinical
chirp of syringes

or graduated glassware
being borne away on a tray

and when I look down
into the institute's garden
I can see the way the pine trees
are standing in two petrified rows to

preen in the cold sunlight,
their needles oiled-looking, polished,
there's a bunk bed in here too,
its red blanket tucked tight—
a soldier's black band of mourning

woven into the wool,
but now you've pulled a chair up to it
and it's turned itself into a refectory table
and I am at a long table behind you and I
call out to you "Did you forget all about me?"

You call back "Yes!" But then you
laugh and I think *But he has bad teeth!*

Because it's by now only too clear that you
take pleasure in turning your back on me,

your voice turns its back on me too,
then turns itself leisurely as you say
to one of the other doctors,
"Tell me about yourself."

It's at this same moment
that I notice how thick
and fat your legs are,

fat sandbags, fat tubes
of liverwurst in their shiny

drawstring casings
of grey-freckled gold skin,

they make me want to
speak of my husband,

make me want
to list you a list
he made for me once—
(all the ways he wanted
me to change)

make me want to say
the sort of banal thing
that, in a dream, one is never
the least bit ashamed to say,

(something about relationships,
something about compromise)

but at this same moment
you turn to look at me
as if you coldly

respect me and then I wake up
and, waking, want to renounce
the dream's desolate logic,

want to say it's only a dream,
want to say it is only filled,
as dreams are, with the irksome

night's flotsam and jetsam,
want not to see the dream as my dream,
want not to see my dream as a dressmaker,

want not to see the way
my dream fell to its knees to

cut and stitch our history
with its rushed alterations.

A BREAST, OUR HEARTS

You could fill a stadium
with the hearts you have broken,
there are rows and rows of us

sitting up here
above the glass beakers,
cunningly tucking a curl
behind a shy ear,

each of us perfumed
for the probing question,

each sundress pocket
with a symptom inside it.

You bring the fascinator's
blaze of your glance
out of your consulting room.

You summon us in,
one at a time.

You love
our love,

you feel our
poised apprehension.

You are
respectful of it.

Clinical as a
lover, you ask the
necessary questions.

We take turns
being worshippers,
perched on the leather
bench across from your desk.

You come around it
to stand close. Like a man
wrapping the wide belt of a
child's kimono for her,

you wrap
the blood pressure cuff

(pneumatic cummerbund)
around a tanned arm,

your gaze
briefly alights

on an embroidered
glimmer of slip.

Sombre and
diagnostic,

you pump
the black bulb,

you pump
the cuff up
for the silent descent,
you watch the numbers

as they pulse
and bop their way down,
we watch you hear the beat

in our blood,
we watch you as if the way

you listen to
our blood's heartbeat

is some kind of
lover's rebuke,

we watch you
as if we would
die for you.

But we could lose
everything here!
A breast,
our hearts!

◆　◆　◆

You call
the next one in,

you look into her eyes,
you hear the faded
cheer going up

in the brazen stadium
of her heart.

You are tactful,
you pretend

not to see it,
not to hear it.

After all,
what we are,
each of us,
what does
it matter?

Not one of us
is too unworthy
to be honoured by pain.

South of the Brain

THE OTHER WOMAN

Everywhere everywhere
tidal squalor—

the great old summer
mansions turned into

clapboard apparitions,
the beach an oil-slicked desert
of bombed sand and driftwood.

But as your car noses its way
into the low grove of weeds

ringing the beach's salted
sand collar we can't wait to

pay our respects to the
clean morning's
burning air.

We tumble out, breathing it in,
and it right away snatches

and skips
our words out to sea.

"Does the sea ever get seasick?"

She is hanging between us,
your youngest daughter, her feet
jacked up into the swinging
crouch of a monkey.

You say that it did once.
"It got too wild and it slapped
itself around and then
it got seasuck."

Seasuck! She shrieks this,
playing the old clown-and-audience
game of father and daughter,

then twists her hands
out of the perch of our hands
and butts her head hard
into my jeaned knee.

"You go away now!
You!" she shrieks at me,
sucking all of the breath out
from under the heart

her own more savage heart
tells her it is only wisdom to injure.

Your eyes, quick and dark for me,
tell me it's only this: the old triangle,
or else she's sniffed the taint of guilt
in our tenderness for her.

Today she is wearing her
navy peacoat with the admiral
buttons and lifts her knees high

to stamp her shining boots
hard down into hard sand.

Now she reaches up with both hands
to grab your fist and swing from it,
crouched bell on a rope

and you start to lope with her
down the long ruin of wet stones,
a one-man merry-go-round,

running and spinning
as she keeps

dipping and rising:

is the sea, is the horse,
is the child, is the rider,

while her triumphing
screams are more and more

drowned out by the drowsy
smash of the cold ocean

IN THE CARDS

In my dream,
lost and blind,
I had to find
my way home
down your face,

your body.
But it's not
in the cards for me
is what you said

when I asked you
if we could be lovers.

The following
evening

riding home
on the train
to Runnymede Station,

the night factoried,
jewelled,

the fields
bone-cold with frost

industrial lights

flying backwards
past the train's
sealed

breath-hungry
windows, I opened
a novel to a page
where a woman
and her brother

were sitting
in a car in Georgia
on a night of cold rain
and while I was imagining

their car smelling
of rained-on car
smells (as if cars were

invented to give
people who are thinking of
changing their lives

a sad and ringside
view of the rain

endlessly
falling)

the brother
was telling his sister
that he'd just signed up
to go off to the war
in Vietnam.

Don't go,
said his sister.

I have to go,
said the brother,
It's in the cards.

What cards,
said his sister.

You know,
said the brother,
The *cards*.

◆   ◆   ◆

I am here
to tell you
he did not
come back

SOUTH OF THE BRAIN

A woman and her two young sons
study the pictures in the Complete
Illustrated Medical Handbook, *bedtime,*
sometime before the year 2,000

Here is the
antlered uterus,

presiding over
the urinary bladder,

presented to the
reader as a

plump purple onion

two inches below
the hunter's wineskin

whose juices are
mixing themselves up with

somebody's supper, and the kidneys,
that pair of boxer's mitts,

one poised on each side
of the bone pole of the spine,

but all of them
far to the south of the brain,

not presented here
as a cauliflower,

as is customary
in books of this sort,
but as what appears to be
a labyrinth in foam rubber.

It's with this same
labyrinth—lulled,

on a night of spring rain,
by an after-bath decorum—

that you recall the lonely
vigil of two brother wolves

racing across
the tops of white pages
to patrol twilight-

steeped snow-maps,

iced mould at the heart
of a dark and violent forest

or the trials
of a lonesome cat
who loses her master

and hunts him down
for nine years

high up in the
tufted and pale wash
of watercolour mountains.

But these are only stories,
only pictures,

you are talcummed
and safe here,

at least until we hear
the bat's claw of a tree branch

against the black window
and look up to see

my childhood making
a bow to your childhood
through the wet glass
and we all get afraid.

ALWAYS THE NOISE THE NIGHTS I AM ALONE

Always the noise the nights
I am alone (the swish of a long
dress or rodent) comes when
some much more sane sound
chooses this same moment
to compete with it:

on the heels
of a stopped rustle

behind the sofa
a flutter in the heart
of the refrigerator motor

so that I listen and listen,
longing for it to repeat itself
so I can name it, willing to

trade frenzied stillness
for a name, a name,

longing for the absolute
silence for diagnosis,

silence in which
there is no bird in a
brief panic beneath the
cold white door's louvred motor,

no discreet click
on linoleum, no click
with the ghost of a claw in it—

no clock's
tick and topple
in the small white plastic sack
stuffed with eggshells and peelings.

For what is a wrong rustling
in the too oddly populated silence
but a thoughtful,

frightful sifting

too carefully calibrated
to dovetail to how little
you were expecting to hear it?

And the terror on both sides
of the wainscotting

(for you, for the rustler)

so that you have no choice
but to pray you could peel the fear
from fear with a paring knife,

peel your way down to the pure core
of what's safe, what might be relied on,

now and forever,
world without end,
amen, but no, it's not that simple—

for what is my life
on a night like tonight
but a history of bargains?

Years and years
of trying to impress
God by showing affection
to the children of others
as a way to guarantee

safe passage through
all of life for my own children,
a thousand and one grudges

given up for the guarded journey
of a husband on his way back
from the city on one of the

rain-slicked nights
of our children's childhood—

the car taking a quick
skip to the left

down one of the wet evening's
highways but then the

world wrenched right
by a tired man in a raincoat,
to say nothing of the years
and years of safe passage
for certain chosen friends
and relations

in exchange
for prayers that were
nothing more than held
breath or cringing.

But these are the true prayers,
the prayers of the body—only the
marketplace of the big bed
by the night window,

sheets blotched with red poppies
and the damp poppies of love
could hold them at bay

for an hour or two. All those
fine old trades and bargains of night,
all of them behind me now:

whose turn to plunder
whose turn to be tender

◆ ◆ ◆

You miss all that?
I miss it.
All the same, you like living alone?
I do. I do like it. My books, my sunlight. My
life. To do as I will with it.
But you're afraid of something?
A noise in the night.
Why does this frighten you so?
It means I can't always be safe.
Why does this bother you?
I don't want to die.
Are you afraid you'll die in pain?
In pain, yes, in the middle of the night.
What else?
The old story.
Which is?
No one to turn to.

IN THE DARK

Coming into my apartment
last night after the party, I was
met by the thought of you everywhere.
I walked from one room to another and
remembered coming back from a party in
another city years ago, years before I knew you.
The man who drove me home was Russian or
half-Russian and so lost in thought that I
became a child again, buttoned into
a half-frightened shyness
beside him.

Each of us
strapped alone to
a tipped leather seat
in the wind, we flew past
the shinto shrine lookout

above the blown Ottawa River
at one o'clock on a cloudy Friday
morning, flew past the rock gardens
with their lily-pad terraces
of petrified stone,

their thousand flower-
regiments guarding a night sweetness
up on those bitten hills in the dark. We
might have been riding in Russia
in an open carriage on the

warm cloudy night
of a more acceptable century.

But I was in love with someone
on that night too. I remember, even
though by then things had turned impossible
between us, letting myself into the sleeping

house and going from room to room,
thinking of him and how,
beneath thinking,

I was swamped
by a quiet that seemed
to have too much history in it
for it to be

felt by
only one person.

I'll tell you a dream
I had in that place:

someone saying someone
was sitting at her
gloom, weaving.

It seemed strange to me last night,
remembering this, because these
last weeks, thinking of you, I
haven't been able to recall

being in love
before you, ever.

I came into the dark
apartment like someone
coming into a house of bad luck.
But the bad luck was after all
outside, in the clear night,
with the wind playing its
dry winter tricks

up among
the crouched
leaves of the trees.
I thought: I should
not have gone out!

It did not seem
after all to have been
what I wanted to do,
to have lost so
many hours of

being here
missing you. I thought,
These are the rooms where I
learned to become tender toward
your absence, these are the rooms
where you have been thought of more
than anyone has been thought of
by anyone, ever.

I walked into the kitchen
and saw in an elbow of light
a list taped to the door
of a cabinet:

almonds
paper clips
Camay soap
envelopes
Write N (don't forget)

I looked
hard at the phone
to see if it had spent
even only a
small part of
the evening ringing

and I remembered a list
I wrote you in a letter once:

your mouth
your body
your seriousness
your crabbiness

(This is true, I wrote,
at least up to a point)
your kindness
your emotion

THE TEACHER'S STORY

Thrill and rush
of your laughter,

I heard it again
tonight, hours after

I'd drawn the curtains
against the city's

light-pricked
heaped twilight.

I smiled at the memory
of it, praised myself for it,
kept smiling to myself as I
locked the door to the balcony,
brushed my hair for the night.
I thought: *I love my class
and my class loves me,
they adored that story,
they were wild about it.*

The way that you laughed! So quick,
so ready! But these were the
dangerous words—*quick, ready*—

these were the words
all my self-congratulation
had been leading me to, the words
that made me realize

you'd heard (because I'd told)
the story before. Your laughter seemed to me
then to have been like the laughter of courtiers,
too quick to acknowledge some mild little
story told by the queen. Or like actors

playing courtiers, actors who've read the part
of the stage-directions where it says *they laugh*.
I turned out the lights and sat on the sofa
in my nightgown in the evening's

swarming and light-flocked dimness,
my hairbrush in my lap. (I was sitting
beneath the leopard poster—

the great cat's body
a cagey rippling of spots,

butterfly's wing of black dots
under each white-furred cat's eye—

code of dots
within a greater code,

like a small but insistent sorrow
cunningly programmed into pleasure.)

I felt as if something
in me had died,

cornered in a
too-bright public place.
I recalled the weather last fall:

the mist and the rain
in the mist, the fine skin
of rain and wet leaves

on the road into the campus;
driven tents of leaves

making shaggy
ankle-gauntlets
to give shelter

to the stone paws of the lions

guarding the flight
of steps up to the east
wing of Stong Hall.

My first year
as a teacher came back to me,

the warning notes I would write
in a savage rush to myself

before walking, white
as surrender, into a seminar room:

N.A. (No anecdotes!)
D.T.T.S.S.O.A.O. (Don't tell the same story
over and over!) D.T.A.S.A.Y. (Don't tell
any stories about yourself!)

Stories like this story:
I am in the Black Forest with
my husband and bees

crawl into our knapsack, and my
husband jumps onto our motorcycle
yelling, "Run with the knapsack,
run behind me! We have to force them
to scatter!" and the bees and I are
flying behind him and I'm crying out,
"Hurry—we must escape before they catch up
with us!" But at the very moment I cry it,

a policeman

pops out from
behind a wall like the wall
of a stage-set to shriek *"Achtung!"*

and we do, and then he
orders me to open the knapsack
and yank out all our mildewed
socks and damp sweaters—the bees

(swarming and German)

having already fled
in a brilliant skyward

exodus up to the leafy camouflage
of a tall avenue of trees,

But now *Achtung*
flies out of the past to sting
and remind me: *Let this word be a warning.*
The last time I spoke it—telling the bee
story on a cloudy morning last April—

I glanced to the far
end of the table to startle
one of you in the act of exchanging
a look with H., caught in his smiling
Tuesday crouch to my left.

Proving what? Proving
I'd forgotten to remember
my fierce list. Proving the medium
of exchange for foreign currencies varies:

> the kopek
> the ruble
> the yen
> the pound
> the smirk
> the look

I forgot all the good times;
forgot the way sometimes when I

meet one of you going up
one of the staircases my heart
is ignited by the rush of something
that looks like love in your eyes,
sweet as the rush of love in the

faces of my own children, long ago.
I forgot the way, in December,

you give me back the words
I spoke in September, but somewhat
more elegantly put than I put them myself.

All I could think was: If only
you knew your own power! If
only you knew how easily your smiles

     (exchanged)

can rip the rug out
from under the tightly
inflated and always too
hopeful balloon of my heart

MORE SAFETY THAN THE
WORLD CAN EVER GIVE

Notes to M. P. on her portfolio for Fiction Workshop Hu 5862B *

There's a time to speak,
and a time not to speak,
and when you came up to
speak (to me) just after the
last class before Christmas,
when you told me you must
have an A, your whole life
depended on it, when you said
you believed in "being upfront
about things," I too should have
spoken, should have said something
teacherly, should have said
"What you don't earn will never
be of any value at all to you",
but instead, under cover of being
flustered, I chose not to speak,
chose not to be a teacher,
chose to be silent,

chose to be a writer and so
just another voyeur of corruption,

chose even to take refuge
in the desolate thought: So *this*
is how the wrong people
get where they get!

As for your portfolio,
and in particular as for
the use of the anthropomorphic
in fiction, we discussed
it several times in class
and I did point out that writers
use it at their peril, but then

there are, after all,
really two kinds of literary
anthropomorphism:

the good kind, the bad kind,
and while the good kind, at least
to my way of thinking, symbolizes man's
(or woman's!) comic/humble relation to the

world, to the elements
("The storm pursued him.....")
the bad kind tends to symbolize
a relationship between an object
and an object—as in, to borrow

from one of the vignettes
in your own portfolio—"The
lace of the girl's silver dress
kissed the sand by the sea"),
and the problem with the relationship
of the latter to the latter is that
it suggests a somewhat saccharine
and dishonest rendering of the world,
as well as a belief system that

insists on more sweetness
and safety than the world
can ever give. Although here
I can't help but recall an
example to undermine

everything I've just said—
do you remember the day I read
from the work of the Swedish poet?
The poem about the houses, late at night,

stepping out into
the headlights—the houses
being awake now and wanting
a drink? It was snowing that day,

snow falling on foggy angora,
on brown and tan plaids,
most of you had come walking
across the campus from Founders
in the spring snow and mud,
although there were some who
would have been only too happy
to alchemize that weather
into the sophomore's
prized elements
of snow and blood—

Not that you were ever
among the bloodhounds.

Far from it. In fact,
overall, there are still
problems with a great deal
of editorial and emotional
control here—a tendency in both
scene-setting and dialogue
(and a tendency which you perhaps
don't even wish to remedy) to
make the world into a world that

doesn't breathe as it should.
The way I would evaluate your
work for the whole year is

in the C range,
a gift, really,
for at this
very moment

I can't help
but remember the way,
for two or three weeks
after the fragrant
and double-edged
season, belled wreath

nailed to the side door
of the north entrance to Ross,
spring winds here and there
seeded with an escaped flake of snow,
you'd chaperone me on a quick walk
across the cold field to Founders,
discussing all the while your impossible A,
while I, like a mother who says to a daughter
"Looks don't matter," said to you
"Marks don't matter", and you
gazed at me with that skeptical
and astounded disappointment
that is the specialty
of the young.

I'd picture you then
as you'd look most Tuesdays
and Thursdays in the workshop,

fair hair tied back
with a demure whip
of leather,

plump knees neatly
tipped to make a good girl's A,

toes pigeon-toed
in your high-fashion
high boots,

small sour smile
propped up on your fists,

forever the one to call
the worst work the best work,
forever the one to defend all clichés!

All of which brings me,
looking back over your portfolio,
to feel a teacher's despair. But there's

also the teacher's legal and vengeful
pleasure (*I was not wrong! I am not wrong!*)
in discovering that there is yet
more kissing—on page 38,
the cover of a book is folded over
until it kisses the back of the book.

I would also like to say
(but should not) that when you
are filling out the Course Evaluation Sheets,
I expect you to be the one to judge me
most harshly. And do you know why?

Because in your stories
you write only of sweetness!

People in your stories
do nothing but smile!

People (and objects!)
do nothing but smile and kiss!

* the initials M.P. are invented initials

On Behalf of the Air

ITS PLEADING GLITTER

For my mother in 1993;
notes on glazing days
in a more innocent decade

There's the hiss
of the bisque

the days she shakes back
her long hair, then ties
her rubber apron
on over her swimsuit

to plunge
everything porous

bubblingly down
into tubs of clear water,
then the almost-hiss
of her quick intake of breath
before she forces each bowl
again all the way down,

but this time the descent
is made in clean silence
as the bowl is tipped in,
then bathed by a more
deadly batter.

Arms gloved by glaze,
arms plunged deep into
basins of poison milk,
or so I imagine as I race
through the Glazing Room
calling out to her:
May I have an orange?
And again, 10 minutes later:
May I have another orange?

I eat 11 or 12 oranges
on windy afternoons in July,
sky blown in from meadow,
glaze dust like ashes
or house dust

falling onto
oranges,

stinging
juice of oranges

tasting of their
sweet networks of pulp

and a tart
hint of metal,

glazes made out of feldspar
and flint and lead oxide
and whiting,

which is why, really,
I'm writing this down here,
I'm so wanting to say:

I know what lead does,
I know what it did
to my mother,

lead rearranged
her spine for her,
lead made her, finally,
four inches shorter,

lead gave her palsy,
lead gave her the shakes,

lead gave her pain,
her eyes are so young with it,

pain with its peculiar,
its pleading glitter,

(and I can't seem to
stop thinking of how
in my bones I'm her daughter)

all of this
reminding me
that after we
moved the Glazing Room

out of the house
and across the misted
field to the Work Barn,

after we turned it
back into a room where
we baked ham and pancakes
instead of teacups
and saucers,

after we hung sunlight
in every tall window,

we breathed in whole
breakfasts of lead,

never once hearing the
shocked hiss of the future,

but then, if we'd heard it,
we'd only have thought it was
the cheerful hiss of the
bisque sucking up

the world's perfect water

LOVE AFTER A LONG ABSENCE (OF LOVE)

Cold day,
too cold to snow,
and as I step into your
hotel a woman hunched up
into fox fur and expensively
fearful with fashion

pushes her way
into the revolving
door's swing with a wince.
The hard light of this city
hurts her eyes while

what's left of the world's
exhaust-fumed and exhausted
but still hurtful late-morning light

makes my own eyes go briefly
blind in the lobby's gold-clocked
vacuumed darkness. I hurry across
its sunless interior, feel my high-
heeled boots sink and spring
in the ruby bog of hotel carpet,

try to calm myself by thinking
of practical things—the food
you said you would buy when we
talked on the phone before lunch:

cold cuts, seedless grapes,

I picture sliced skirts of ham,
hemmed by white borders of fat,
iridescent silken thin pink layers
of ham, tasting of cloves
and spiced grease.

All this an excuse for the wine
which we joked on the phone
I would certainly need.

All that tenderness for my
embarrassment, as if we were

parents and my embarrassment
our child and it gave us pleasure
to smile down at it together.

But a man waiting at the elevator
reminds me of you in some more
heartless incarnation. His glance

bleak with disinterest, he
buttons his coat all the way up to his eyes.

We rise fifteen floors together
in unmoored silence.

The shock of the new,
somebody said that about
something once—art, maybe,
but it makes me think
of you, I see you as a baby,

puffin-chested, boss-baby,
king of everyone in the sandbox.

But now the elevator doors
part for me, silken steel,
accommodating, ominous,

I find a tall mirror
that's willing to stand still for me,
damp-palmed, I smooth down my skirt,

my heart, last Thursday night
I could have sworn I saw you

kissing someone with a tall throat
in a car, you were wearing the

pristine white shirt of a
betrayer, your tie loosened,

your arm long
along the back of the seat

while your friend tilted her head back
into the shelter of your armpit,

her heart and mouth
and every part of her open,

I felt jolted sick
by what I saw (or thought I saw)
and at the same time swamped by the
memory of that heavenly

moment in cars when men
become so male, so maternal,

I hurried past the car's
mud-studded wheels,

ill with desire and envy I was
convinced that the man in the white shirt
foreshadowed our end,

I was even convinced he had to be you,
but how could he have been you,

in a car not your car,
in a city not your city,
and at that time of the night?

I DREAM OF THE AFTERLIFE

Walking among all the cars
and the dainty joggers,

I dream of the afterlife,

picture Heaven
as an auto-free city,

picture idlers and polluters,
after the marriage between Hell and Hell,

tied like tin cans to the back doors
of the cars of the damned—

Let them be wreathed in (and breathe in)
exhaust fumes forever!

I cross to the traffic-islanded
park, hurry through a glade

hung with a brief
fog of diesel,

pass the bricked-in bile
of the park's lagoon
of dead water, pass
under the high

spin and polish
of the innocent sky

while miniature flowers
sweet as choirs or tiny eyes

keep looking down from their
grandstands of lawn

far from the childhood air
of Bald Mountain, untamed,

fragrant
sting of it,

up among the wild pinks
of the roses, and it's
not just the bad air, either,
but the language—the dismantling of logic—

the host on the breakfast show
this morning saying, "And I'd like
to thank all you good people who
called in with your camping memories,
past, present and future—"

Tell me, all you good people
out there in Radio Land,

do you remember
the excavated aroma of the coffee

we used to drink
up under the pine trees?

Seashells
cracked like eggshells

on the cold path to the beach?
The way we all used to

run down the
spine of the pure morning?

Québec, Canada
1997

SIGNAL EDITIONS POETRY SERIES
Edited by Michael Harris

Visit Véhicule Press on the Web...

http://www.cam.org/~vpress